To:
Marlene—
Hope you enjoy
the book + thanks
for your support.
Love,
—Peggy—

AS FAR AS

AS FAR AS EYE CAN SEE

2912 Candelaria Dr.
Henderson, NV 89074

EYE CAN SEE

poems by Peggy Ruesch

drawings by Dawn Humphries

Printed by Cedar Mountain Publishing

Jacket Design by Dawn Humphries

Printed in the United States of America

First Edition

Library of Congress Cataloging and Publication Data
Ruesch, Peggy
As Far As Eye Can See

ISBN # 0-9724168-0-3

For Synjyn, Guinness and Courtney

Crazy Critters

I followed a tarantula
And poked it with a stick.
I chased a dozen rabbits
But they ran really quick.

I squeezed a preying mantis
He didn't pray at all.
I teased some pretty ladybugs
Climbing up the wall.

I pulled a baby lizzard's tail
He squirmed and got away.
I've really had a swell time
With these critters here today.

Good grief, I'm in a pickle
So I'll hoof it to this tree--
Cause all those critters I annoyed
Are rightly chasing me!

1

Mr. Lodell

Oh Mr. Lodell, the stories you tell
Your tales are quite off the wall.
You traveled the west with a badge on your chest
Making all of the bank robbers fall.

You hunted a snake in a freezing cold lake
It measured a hundred feet long.
Rode down the Nile on a mean crocodile
Laughing and whistling a song.

Sailed the blue sea with two pirates or three
Flew the Red Baron at night.
Slayed a green dragon with it's tongue still a waggin'
Then smiled when you took your first bite.

Found treasures of gold in a cave filled with mold
You fought with the Three Musketeer's.
Crossed the Sahara in a robe and tiara
Chasing camels for twenty-three years.

Oh Mr. Lodell, the stories you tell
You were good to the rich and the poor.
Your tales may be tall and quite off the wall
But I beg you--please tell me one more.

Rover Had Fleas

Rover had a bunch of fleas
So on a Springtime day,
We picked through Rover's matted fur
But they wouldn't go away.

We knew this was a hairy job
So we called our kinfolk in.
My grandma got real nauseous
While my grandpa picked and
grinned.

Everyone was picking fleas
Til they could pick no more,
And there were forty piles at least
Heaped on the kitchen floor.

Rover looks a bit hysterical
Since the fleas all left our hound.
Now he fits through the doggie door
Cause he's just one inch around.

Nice Hippopotamus

Don't tell a hippopotamus
She's way too big to ride a bus.

Don't tell her that her hips are big
Don't say her hair looks like a wig.

Don't tell a hippopotamus
She shouldn't cook and make a fuss--

Cause she'll whip up a gourmet meal
Of wet eyeballs and spoiled veal.

Don't mention you don't like her food
Because she'll think you're very rude.

Just let her do what she will do
or you'll be squished when she sits
on you.

Ghosts

I'm sure ghosts are hiding
Right under my bed,
And when dad leaves the room
They'll pounce on my head.

There's thirty at least
All piled under there.
Twenty-nine are bald-headed
And one's got some hair.

There's short ones and tall ones
Some fat and some thin.
One ghost is real spooky
With a half crooked grin.

6

Please stay with me dad
Until I fall asleep.
I won't blink an eyelash
Or make one little peep.

Dad sang lots of songs
Til way after three.
What a great pal he was
To stay there with me.

I was almost asleep
When I heard a loud noise.
Ghosts were under my bed
Tripping over my toys.

Then I heard one ghost say,
"My poor ears are ringing
With these corny songs
And that lousy singing."

The last words he spoke
As I heard them all flee--
"Let's split! All these songs
Are too scary for me!"

The Big Pimple

My sister was a basket case
With a giant pimple on her face.
She stormed around the house all day
And sulked without a word to say.

She hid way underneath her bed
And threw a blanket on her head.
She wouldn't answer her blue phone
And refused to give our dog a bone.

She covered it up with a huge band-aid
Cause she was upset and really afraid--
That people would notice her big pimple
On her forehead above her dimple.

She moped around and wanted to cry
"What's wrong with a pimple?" I said on the sly.
"My life will be ruined forever I guess.
There's pus in this pimple and I'm a big mess."

Her best friend came over and whispered a sigh
"I'll bet with that pimple you just want to die!"
"Nonsense," she said, "please don't ramble on.
By morning this pimple will be dried up and gone!"

Seven Red Ants

Seven red ants in matching plaid pants
Joined the circus in town,
Swung on a trapeze with interlocked knee's
Then performed with Jeppo the clown.

Seven red ants in matching plaid pants
Rode pyramid on a white pony,
Said one of the ants, "We are taking a chance
Cause our legs are so wobbly and bony."

Seven red ants in matching plaid pants
Were in the height of their glory,
But a rainstorm one day blew those poor ants away
And that is the end of their story.

Seven red ants vanished in a quick glance
For they got washed away in the rain,
But inside that tent where the rain came and went
One small pair of plaid pants remain.

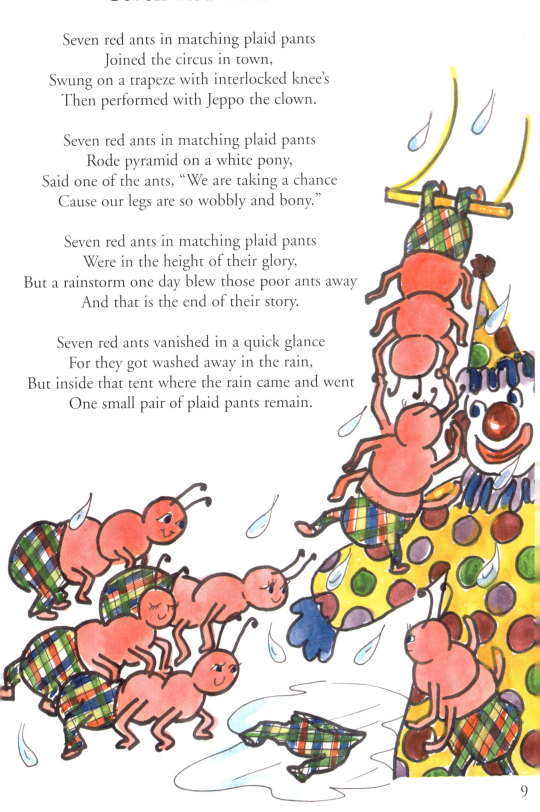

My Shiny Go-Cart

I won a shiny go-cart
In a contest from my town,
And when I jumped inside it
The pedal hit the ground.

I put my trusty helmet on
Because I was no fool,
Driving around my neighborhood
Looking really cool.

"Let us have a ride in that"
Hollered Mark and Pete,
But I accelerated really fast
As I flew down the street.

Mrs. Johnson's pretty flowers
Got "mowed down" as they say,
But maybe they will bloom again
On another springtime day.

Sweet young Jenny waved at me
With groceries on her arm,
I had no time to help her out
But I know she loved my charm.

I ran over seven garbage cans
And some potted roses too--
Gosh, I really dig this go-cart
Of bright metalic blue.

Things looked like a whirlwind
Everywhere I went,
And baby Michael's yellow trike
Got a tiny little dent.

Heck, I was in a hurry
And I really did look cool,
But strangely no one talked to me
The next day at my school.

My friends turned up their noses
As I gobbled up my food,
And I just kept on wondering
Where they got their attitude.

Yes, I really got the brush off
From all the kids that day,
But I'm still really puzzled--
Why my friends all went away.

Mishap Snowman

We made a funny snowman
Used a pickle for his nose.
We used pretzels for his buttons
And flippers for his toes.

Found a tattered cowboy hat
And stuck it on his head.
We found some cool sunglasses
And a checkered vest of red.

We liked our funny snowman
So we bundled him up tight.
Brought him into the kitchen
And stayed with him all night.

He really did seem magical
So we served him raisin bread,
Then took a fluffy dish towel
And wiped his sweating head.

We fed him some hot cocoa
Then poured him two cups more,
Now all that's left of snowman
Is a puddle on the floor.

Grandma's Braid

"Fiddle dee dee," my grandma said,
"I cannot find my glasses.
Sit down and I will braid your hair
So you won't miss your classes."

I tried to tell my grandma
That I didn't want a braid,
But she didn't understand me
Without her hearing aid.

"Sit still." she said, "You wiggle worm
Don't try to run away.
I told your mother I'd help out
And fix your hair today."

I hollered and I yelped out loud
But grandma kept on brushing,
Then grandpa came into the room
And I couldn't stop from blushing.

I'll not deny her braid was good
But here's the real twister--
She braided up her grandson's hair,
Cause she thought it was his sister!

Imagine

Imagine a ride on a big ferris wheel,
And as it goes round you make a big squeal.

Imagine it circling nine times at least,
After pigging way out on a huge pizza feast.

Imagine the fun I am having with Joe,
Waving and shouting to the people below.

Imagine Joe sitting right next to me,
With cut off pants and a scraped up knee.

Imagine I'm sick--my face is dark green,
I think I better get off this machine.

Imagine--hooray! I'm feeling like new,
I just threw up on Joe's tennis shoe.

Imagine him mumbling, "I hope you had fun,
Cause when this ride is over--you better run."

Pitiful Bird

Have you ever heard of a pitiful bird
Who never quite learned how to fly?
He looks rather weird with his tail feathers sheared
And his neck stretching up to the sky.

That pitiful bird was a poor clumsy nerd
When he tried to ascend to the sky.
He learned how to cook and wrote a nice book
Then dressed in a white shirt and tie.

Went off to college to gain lots of knowledge
Ended up with a Master's Degree.
Built a big house with a two-headed mouse
Then taught his grandmother to ski.

Cut hair in the Navy and ate lumpy gravy
Invented some polka dot cheese.
Rescued some people stranded high in a steeple
And cured a dreaded disease.

Have you ever heard of a pitiful bird
Who couldn't ascend to the sky?
My word, my word, what a pitiful bird
Who never quite learned how to fly.

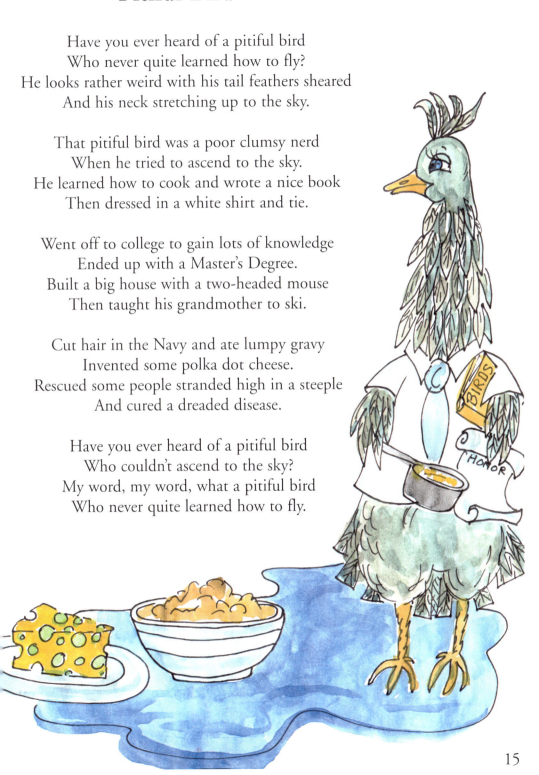

15

Cowboy Carl

Cowboy Carl was bad and mean
With a beard black as the night.
He packed a pistol on his hip
And was ready for a fight.

He wore a patch on his left eye
Had a gold-capped shiny tooth,
But if you knew he told a lie
You'd pretend he told the truth.

Yea, he was mean and ugly
Yet all the townfolk knew,
Not to look him in the eye
Or he'd sniff you down like glue.

His clothes were soiled and smelly
Didn't use a lot of soap.
He'd spit upon his leather boots
Then hang 'em on a rope.

One evening Carl came ridin' in
Back to his mamma's place--
She snapped, "You're way past curfew."
He saw her angry face.

"Now git inside and go ta bed."
Then she twisted up his ear,
And he felt like a kid again
In all that cowboy gear.

He was really tough as nails
But not in mamma's eye's--
She was barely four feet tall
And Carl was twice her size.

He slinkied to his bedroom
Just like a naughty pup.
He whined, "I won't be late again"
Then filled her coffee cup.

Now when curfew comes around
And he's out stirrin' trouble,
He don't want ta make his mamma mad--
So he gits home on the double.

17

Yucky Veggies

Every night at dinnertime
She'd put veggies on my plate,
And I would watch my family
Chatting while they ate.

They'd eat squash and carrots
Brussel sprouts and peas,
But they turn my stomach inside out
And give me wobbly knees.

I'll eat some meat and noodles
Or casseroles I suppose,
But I don't like those veggies
They wrinkle up my toes.

Fido sure looks hungry
I'll feed him one small pea,
And just a bit of spinach
So he'll get strong like me.

I will feed him every night
Cause I'm sweet to the core,
But I'll be very careful
Not to spill them on the floor.

I really wouldn't CARROT all
And not TURNIP my nose,
If mother never LETTUCE
Eat a single one of those.

Fido loves to eat my veggies
He is a boy's best friend,
And I will surely love him
Until the very end.

Last night while we were eating
And after grace was said,
Dad put Fido on his lap
Then gently stroked his head.

I really howled with laughter
When dad fell for the bait,
He mumbled, "I can't figure out
How Fido's gained this weight."

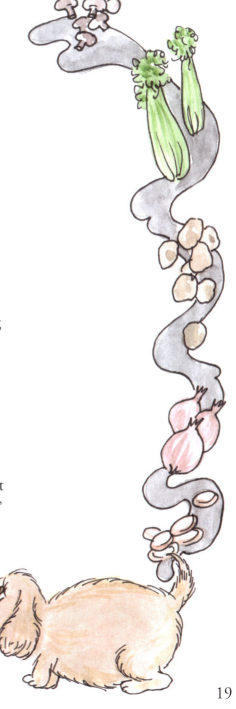

Really Artificial

She took her contact lenses out
And her fake eyelashes too,
Then one by one peeled off her nails
Held on with tacky glue.

She lifted off her wiglet
Took out her teeth so white,
Then wiped her bright red lipstick off
And she really looked a fright.

Her husband Mel came walking in
His face was full of strife.
"Excuse me ma'am." he bleakly said
"I'm looking for my wife."

So if you paint and powder
And take out all your teeth,
Make sure folks know it's really you--
That's hidden underneath.

The Little Fiddler

She practiced on her fiddle
But had no way of knowing,
That when she picked her fiddle up
The flowers all stopped growing.

Her dog would howl and hide his head
But she felt really proud,
Cause she loved to play her fiddle
Though she screeched it really loud.

Grandpa put some earmuffs on
Then blasted the TV,
But she just kept on thinking
This sounds awfully good to me.

She blew the roof right off the house
And shattered all the glass,
The water tank exploded
And watered all the grass.

Her house was ripped to pieces
And beneath that hardwood floor,
The termites who resided there
Packed up and moved next door.

21

So Many Cookies

I can juggle twenty cookies
Standing on my head,
And I've got hoards of cookies
Underneath my bed.

I've got them in the living room
Stacked up by my chair,
And some are on my dresser
Where I comb my curly hair.

A gingersnap or macaroon
Are ones I love by far,
I've even stashed some Oreo's
In the glove box of our car.

I really do love cookies
And I'd really like to be,
A taster in a factory
With those cookies next to me.

I'd gobble every cookie
Because each one is yummy,
But I really love them best of all
When they're sitting in my tummy.

Beauty Shop Chatter

They used a sterling silver brush
To get through her tangled hair.
She stood in total silence
But sat not in the chair.

A fancy little braid was done
Tied off with colored bows.
She got the special treatment
From her head down to her toes.

A squirt or two of lacquer
Held every hair in place,
But when the fumes got in her nose
She made a sour face.

She was a raving beauty
With her silken hair of white,
But no one hardly noticed
She had an overbite.

The other gals all envied her
Cause she looked simply great,
And all of them were wondering
If she was going on a date.

When this glamour gal stepped out
And her escort came to call,
She felt like Cinderella
Going to a ball.

She rode not in a limosine
But a cart with filtered shade,
For she was just a sweet young mare
Riding in the town's parade.

Mr. Grumbles

Old Mr. Grumbles
Lived quietly alone,
Didn't own a TV
A cat or a phone.

Each day he would wear
A mean frown on his face,
Inside his dark house
Just taking up space.

One night during dinner
As he ate all alone,
He whacked his poor elbow
And it tickled his bone.

He tried not to laugh
Because that wouldn't do,
So he held his breath
Until he turned blue.

He started to smile
But out came a laugh,
Then Grumbles poor face
Cracked right in half.

So if you don't smile
And use what you've got,
You might lose it all
right there on the spot!

Dog Day Dance

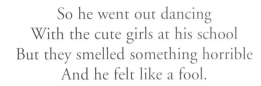

He stepped in doggie doo-doo
But didn't even know it
And if you looked him over
He really didn't show it.

So he went out dancing
With the cute girls at his school
But they smelled something horrible
And he felt like a fool.

Shortly he discovered
That "stuff" was on his shoe
So he hopped out on just one foot
While everyone gasped, "pew!"

The kids all held their noses
And stuck a pointing finger.
He was gone without a trace
But how that smell did linger.

Two months later he returned
And looking really cool
Strutted out onto the dance floor
To impress the girls at school.

He was having quite a time
Til they yelled, "We know you!
You're the kid that ran around
With doo-doo on your shoe!"

So the moral of this story is
If you go out to a dance
Check yourself from head to toe
And do not take a chance--

That you will be remembered
Which is very sad, but true
Going to the dance one night
With doo-doo on your shoe!

Poor Iguana

A young girl named Shaunna squished an iguana
Then simmered it nice and slow.
She savored each bite well into the night
From her head to the tip of her toe.

It had a great taste and none did she waste
Except for the eyeballs and feet.
Her dog ate them up like a starved little pup
And her cat froze right there in his seat.

At quarter 'til two her face turned all blue
Then she felt something wiggle inside.
She wanted to run for that thing she had done
But instead she just sat down and cried.

Then in a big flash she made a mad dash
To the doctor--screaming like mad.
She puked up it's chin and pieces of skin
Sobbed again and felt horribly bad.

Now dear little Shaunna if you eat an iguana
That's covered with scales and slime--
Be very aware as you sit in your chair
To chew it up better next time!

What Things Ain't

I'm glad I am an artist
The world is mine to paint,
And with a magic line or curve
I make things what they ain't.

I can paint an orange zebra
A turquoise polar bear,
An ostrich with some polka dots
Or a turtle with some hair.

I'm glad I am an artist
It's fun to be in charge,
I can draw a tiny hippo
Or make a green ant large.

Six brightly colored aliens
Are dressed in hula skirts,
And monsters with antenna's
Are wearing flowered shirts.

Rats--here comes my brother
He's quite a pest I fear,
So I'll take my big eraser
And make him disappear.

Sweet Alice Marie

There once was a girl
Named Alice Marie,
Who did everything
Quite haphazardly.

She'd brush her teeth
With Ivory soap,
Then tie up her shoes
With a forty-foot rope.

She'd plant lots of seeds
When there was no sun,
Then drink scrambled eggs
When she was all done.

Sweet Alice Marie
Your garden is quaint,
But if anyone saw it
I'm sure they would faint.

I love all those turnips
And your roses of red,
But why is your garden
On **top of your head?**

That Crazy Yak

Have you ever seen a yak
Who tried like heck to scratch his back?

Or have you ever seen a yak
Blowing up a paper sack?

Have you seen a purple yak
With polka dots of green and black?

Now did you ever see a yak
Conversing with his buddy Jack?

Have you ever seen a yak
Dancing with a carpet tack?

Have you ever seen a yak
Who ran away and would not come back?

I have NEVER seen a yak
With polka dots of green and black.

But if I do, I'll surely see--
A yak doesn't mean that much to me!

Tate The Great

Once I had a little flea
Who acted like a king.
I bought him fancy clothes and hats
And a shiny diamond ring.

I taught him how to do a dance
And how to sing a song.
He even learned some funny jokes
But didn't take him long.

He could brush his sharp white teeth
And braid his flowing hair.
He learned to juggle twenty balls
With one leg in the air.

He had to have the perfect name
So I came up with Tate.
He was such a brilliant flea
I called him Tate The Great.

Then I started thinking
We could be a real hot team.
We'd move out to Hollywood
And that would be a dream.

We could make a fortune
Split the money right in half,
Because a flea with all those jokes
Would surely get a laugh.

We made up a great routine
So it would be just right.
We practiced every morning
and every single night.

I packed his tiny sequined shirts
And denim coat of blue,
Then we set off to make it big
To see our dream come true.

I slipped him in my pocket
He felt so warm and snug.
What an awesome team we made
Just me and little bug.

The day was hot, I was dry
And so was little flea.
We hopped inside a local pub
To have a glass of tea.

On the table stood my little flea
As the waiter brought our drink.
I was going to show him Tate
But had no time to blink.

He smooshed my flea so quickly
It brought me to my knee's,
He wiped him off and mumbled
"We sure get lots of these!"

Mr. Tim

My grandma had an uncle
His name was Mr. Tim.
All he liked to do each day
Was swim, swim, swim.

He'd swim every single morning
Til very late at night,
Swim when it was cloudy
Or when the sun was bright.

He wouldn't speak to anyone
Didn't live the golden rule.
All he did was swim and swim
Just like a crazy fool.

Meals would hardly touch his lips
He had better things to do.
Grandma said, "You'd better eat
Or there won't be much of you."

The raging winds would come and go
But he kept a grimace grin.
He never stopped for anything
And was getting mighty thin.

Then one day as fate would have
Yes, we still think of him,
He slipped through the drain pipe.
Goodbye, Mr. Tim!

Baby Sister

Got a brand new baby sister
With twinkling eyes of blue,
And as I studied her small face
I wondered--will she do?

She was cute and tiny
But wouldn't be for long,
And I just hoped when she grew up
She'd be big and strong.

She had no teeth nor strand of hair
But I guess that's quite okay,
Because she's got two perfect hands
That are cute in every way.

Now little kids can wonder
And most kids have a dream,
Some take care of baby sisters
And some have got a scheme.

So I'll keep thinking happy thoughts
Then stack up all my wishes--
And I'll be sailing on cloud nine
When she can WASH THE DISHES!

Mean Mean Old Mrs. Frye

Mean mean old Mrs. Frye
Hung her husband out to dry,
Cause she was tired of him a wishin'
That he was on the lake out fishin'.

Poor poor old Mr. Frye
Is hanging on the line to dry,
Some clothespins clipped upon his nose
And blackbirds pecking at his toes.

Mean mean old Mrs. Frye
Never ever wanders by,
To check on him who was a wishin'
That he was on the lake out fishin'.

Lucky lucky old Mr. Frye
Shrunk two sizes when he was dry,
Then slipped out of his clothes one day-
Grabbed his pants and ran away.

Happy happy old Mr. Frye
Never has a tear filled eye,
Cause he is happy as a mole
On the lake with his fishin' pole.

Now if you're dreamin' and a wishin'
That you were on the lake out fishin',
Don't marry a woman like Mrs. Frye
Or she will hang you out to dry.

Lemonade For Sale

Did you ever sell some lemonade
On a summer day out in the shade?
Did just two people stop on by--
Your mom, your neighbor and a pesky fly?

Did you drink tons of lemonade
Til you were sick out in the shade?
Then all day long close to the end
You thought you didn't have one friend.

Your neighbor walked across the grass
Placing his order for a glass.
You poured it full there in the shade
And watched him drink his lemonade.

He winked and gave a friendly sigh
Said, "Lucky me, for coming by.
That's the best lemonade I've tasted by far.
Here's a five dollar tip to go in your jar."

Heck, I didn't know and I couldn't tell
That he liked lemonade that well.
As he wandered off I heard him say,
" Thanks for the mem'ry and have a great day."

I had no idea he liked lemonade
But I'm really thrilled with the money I made.
Now thanks to him I can go off and play
And I certainly will have a really great day.

Smarty Marty

The strangest kid I ever saw
Had beady eyes and hair like straw.

He had a very serious look
And his nose was always in a book.

A special briefcase held his pen
But he slept only now and then.

He was smart as smart could be
And loved to read geography.

There was brilliance underneath
Those horned rim glasses and crooked teeth.

He'd debate a teacher's talk
But he could not chew gum and walk.

I never saw his face again
But heard of stories where he'd been.

He got well known and yesterday
Got put in charge of the C.I.A.!

Freeda The Frog

Freeda the frog was a kindly young gal
Who dwelt on a green lily pad.
Most of her friends lived a short hop away
And so did her great grandpa's dad.

Freeda the frog was a poor sight to see.
She was wartless and her neck was too long.
Her eyes were too small for her big shiny head
But she sang a most beautiful song.

Every night on the green lily pad
She would sing in her angelic way,
Bringing sweet music to others
As she sang til the wee hours of day.

Freeda was homely but folks didn't care
For her countenance sparkled and shined.
She would spread laughter all of the time.
She was pure and gentle and kind.

Once while Freeda was just hanging out
Content on her green lily pad,
She noticed a toad catching some flies
Chatting with her great grandpa's dad.

He seemed all array this magnificent toad
A toad of all toads you might say,
And his eye's were only for Freeda
As he watched her the rest of the day.

There were prettier frogs who lived in the pond
And they couldn't believe their eyes,
That he would pick Freeda above all the rest
To be his most beautiful prize.

"Freeda surely is one in a million,"
The frogs croaked loudly with pride--
"For its not just your outer beauty that counts,
But it's what you've got way deep inside!"

37

Hangin' Out

"We don't want to go to Auntie's house,
Can't we just stay home and play?
It's really, really boring
And it's just too far away."

"Hop in the car," my mother said.
"An hour won't be too long."
We rode across Bonanza Road
And mother hummed a song.

We got to Auntie Mary's house
But we were full of gloom,
Until we spotted something weird
Inside a tiny room.

We picked that really weird thing up
Our faces drew a blank.
What was this stick-like rubber bowl
Next to the toilet tank?

"It" stuck nicely on the ceiling
So my sister hung on tight.
She was pretty lightweight
And we laughed with all our might.

"Let me have a turn." I said
But I crashed down to the floor.
When we were finished laughing,
We laughed and laughed some more.

We really had a good old time
And that house became appealing--
As we hung from the toilet plunger
On Auntie Mary's ceiling.

Qucasy

I will stand beneath this cloud
As it pours down rain,
I don't care if I get wet
I don't feel any pain.

If the snow falls down on me
And turns my nose to blue,
It doesn't make a difference
It's what I want to do.

If some buzzards circle 'round
I guess I'll be their prey,
I won't budge for anything
I'll stay right here all day.

Gosh! I just saw lovely Sara
Swinging on her gate.
Why is my stomach churning?
Is it something that I ate?

Something's taking hold of me
I'm weak with wobbly knee's.
What's going on here anyway
Do I have a rare disease?

I'm feeling very queasy now
My brain's a tangled mess,
My heart is beating wildly
I'm cracking up I guess.

Nothing's making any sense
My thoughts have run amuck.
I think I finally figured out
I'm hopelessly "Love Struck!"

All Over The Place

Rode a train in Central square
Kicked a football in the air.
Played with frogs at Sutter's Lake,
Ate a hot dog and some cake.

Threw my frisbee, took a swim
Shot marbles with my best friend Jim.
Teased some girls to hear them squeal,
Slipped on a wet banana peel.

Rode my bike and played some ball
Watched some bugs climb up a wall.
Bought some worms to use for bait,
And swung on Grandpa Johnson's gate.

Chased a rainbow in the sky
Then tried to see if I could fly.
Climbed a tree and scraped my nose,
And got some blister's on my toes.

Rolled down a hill, picked some clover
Ran and ran the whole day over.
Caught an orange butterfly,
Got some dirt stuck in my eye.

When I got home from all that play
Dad said, "What did you do today?"
I thought real hard as I stood tall,
Then I replied--"Not much at all!"

My Cousin & The Fly

I slumped way down into my seat
Inside the movie theatre.
I didn't fear a six foot snake
Or a creepy alligator.

On the screen in front of me
Was a big ole monstrous fly.
It was making my blood curdle
So I covered up one eye.

I was sure that "thing" would get me
As I yelled a frightful scream.
Oh, how I wish that hairy fly
Was simply just a dream.

My cousin sitting next to me
Let out a thunderous roar,
And when she finally found me
I was crouched down on the floor.

"Get up you boob." she hollered,
"Now sit back in your chair.
Stop acting like a fraidy cat.
It's just a fly with hair."

She was really acting macho
And she laughed until she hurt.
I had goose bumps on my arms
While sweat ran down my shirt.

I'd scream and she'd put up her fist
We were quite a crazy pair,
But I was trying very hard
To stay calm in my chair.

When the movie finally ended
And I went home that night,
I thought about the hairy fly
Then my body shook with fright.

Now I couldn't help but wonder
As I breathed a big long sigh,
Who was I more afraid of--
My cousin or the fly?

41

This Old Quarter

Who wants to buy this quarter?
I'll sell it for a dime.
I've had this quarter in my room
For such a long, long time.

Who wants to buy this quarter?
It won't buy a candy bar.
It won't buy a soda pop
Or a pickle in a jar.

The bank just bought my quarter
Got a dime and three big nickels.
Now I'll buy a candy bar
A soda and two pickles.

Goodbye, ole rusty quarter
You just got old with time.
Now I've got a lot more "cents"
With three nickels and a dime.

What's In A Name?

Daddy calls me Billie boy
But that's okay with me,
Because we are the best of pals
That there could ever be.

Grandma calls me sweetheart
I am her special guy,
And we are thick as whipping cream
On top of chocolate pie.

At school they call me plain ole Bill
Though I'm not too plain at all,
For I love to climb the monkey bars
And play a game of ball.

Mother calls me cutie pie
Pumkin cakes or hon,
And I don't really mind at all
Cause she's just having fun.

Now if I sorted through these names
And picked one for a winner,
Any name would be okay
Just don't call me "late for dinner".

Ole Bean

I burped up a bean
One night during dinner,
And I must admit
It came out a winner.

Next thing I knew
At twenty past five,
That cute little bean
Came wildly alive.

It jumped up and down
On my kid sister's lap,
And stared at my grandma
Who was taking a nap.

It hopped on the table
And onto the chair,
That crazy ole bean
Hopped around everywhere.

My bedroom was loaded
With many a toy,
And it was a ball
For a bean and his boy.

We played with my cars
It beat me at chess,
We had a great time
Though my room was a mess.

We played on my video
And watched my TV,
Read lots of good books
Til way after three.

Without any warning
It was gone in a flash,
So I frantically hunted
Outside in the trash.

I was really depressed
So I searched the place over,
Then checked all the fur
On my little dog Rover.

I miss my ole bean
It was really a winner,
So I'm hoping next week
We'll get chili for dinner.

Flyin' High

Two sore fingers, one bruised shin
Seven stitches on my chin.

Got three cracked ribs, a punctured spleen
When I sprung off my trampoline.

One eyeball is black and blue
I think the other one is too.

You may not think that it made sense
When I jumped off my neighbor's fence.

A bone is cracked inside my hip
My finger's numb out to the tip.

My neck and back have sprung ajar
When I leaped off my neighbor's car.

These broken bones don't hurt at all
And it's okay if I should fall.

But I will wonder every day
If Superman began this way.

Uncle Arthur's Toe

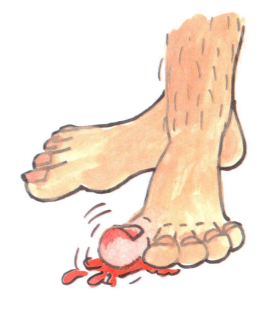

Uncle Arthur stubbed his toe
And blood oozed out all over.
It bled on Auntie Edna's rug
And outside in the clover.

His toe swelled up, turned all black
So he felt really blue.
He was in a lot of pain
And couldn't wear his shoe.

His toe looked really yucky
So people hid their eyes,
And very often he would hear
Some giggles, moans and sighs.

His two feet didn't match at all
He limped on his left side,
But Uncle Arthur was a man
Who had a lot of pride.

Then one day as luck would have
He stubbed his other toe.
He let out a giant squeal
And out the blood did flow.

Auntie Edna darted out
And saw the blood all over.
She saw it on the sidewalk
And you guessed it--in the clover.

Uncle Arthur stood right there
With a grin a mile long.
He was acting really happy
And whistling a song.

In a flash his words came out
As he grabbed his garden hoe,
"I'm not mismatched anymore
Cause I've stubbed my other toe."

47

My Room Is
In Shambles

My room is in shambles
In shambles I fear.
It looks like a freight train
Did havoc in here.

My bike's on the bed
There's a quilt on the floor.
My homework is crumbled
In a pile by my door.

Some crayons and pencils
Are mixed in with a stamp.
My baseball and bat
Are on top of my lamp.

I've got dirty worn socks
Stashed under my chair,
And on top of them all
Is a dust ball with hair.

Got a shoe in my drawer
With a broken shoe lace,
And three wilted sunflowers
In a white plastic vase.

One bit of advice
I feel I must bring -
Don't let mom clean your room
Or you **won't** find a thing.

The Great Divide

We had a shiny nickel
To buy a candy bar.
We walked across the desert
Cause we couldn't drive a car.

We talked about our candy bars
Which one should we buy?
"I think I'd like to try them all"
Came my swift reply.

"Silly girl, you can't do that"
My sister said with pride.
"Pick your favorite candy bar
And then let me divide."

I picked a chocolate gooey crunch
It was the biggest one,
Then I tossed it to my sister
Who was always loads of fun.

She broke it carefully in half
As I gave my lips a smack.
She took a couple bites of mine
Before she gave it back.

I whimpered like a baby
"Gosh, I don't like this game."
She said, "Now don't you worry,
They're divided just the same!"

"Thanks," I said with a cheery smile
"You're really quite a gal."
Then as I ate I had no doubt
She was **MY** best friend and pal!

Mandy & Her Monkey

Mandy had a monkey
She named it Myra Jane,
But Mandy always seemed to think
Her monkey was too plain.

She put curlers in it's hair
Then painted up it's toes,
Clipped on some beaded jewelry
Then powdered up it's nose.

She added bright red lipstick
And a dab of perfume too,
Put rings upon it's fingers
Then lined it's eyes in blue.

When she dressed it in a frilly blouse
Myra flew into a rage,
It made a shreiking high pitched squea
Then hid behind it's cage.

That frilly blouse was ripped and torn
And it was the monkey's ploy--
But I can't say I blame it none
Cause Myra was a boy!

Practice, Practice, Practice

I don't want to practice
These boring old scales,
So I'll probably sit here
And bite off my nails.

These songs about spiders
And white billy goats,
Are really quite silly
And I can't read the notes.

I've practiced these songs
Til I'm blue in the face,
But I'm still sitting here
In this same little space.

My knuckles are stiff
My eyeballs are sore.
My feet are so numb
I can't feel the floor.

I don't want to practice
So there'll be no debate.
The sun has gone down
And it's getting late.

My mom just came in
Saw my arms folded tight,
Asked what I was playing
I replied, "Silent Night."

I Forgot To Remember

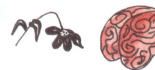

I forgot to remember what I tried to forget.
My brain is all tangled like a twisted up net.

Mailed an unwritten letter that I didn't write.
Wore my sunglasses in the dark of the night.

Waved a great big hello instead of goodbye.
Heard two funny jokes and both made me cry.

I forgot to remember if my left is my right
And during a snowstorm I flew my red kite.

Answered the door when no one was there.
Sat up in my bed and slept in my chair.

It was raining racoons so I hung out my clothes.
Blew my blonde head and polished my nose.

I forgot to remember if I'm forward or back.
I wonder--do flowers grow mostly in black?

My hair's neatly combed with an old garden rake
And I think that I'm snoring while I am awake.

I oiled the cat and put out the fish.
Ate all of my cake then made a big wish.

I forgot to remember what I tried to forget.
My brain is all tangled like a twisted up net.

But one thing's for sure--if I have my way,
Each night will no doubt be a beautiful day.

52

Bullet

My little dog Bullet
Isn't too smart,
But that's fine with me
Cause he's got a big heart.

He's rowdy and gentle
He's sly and he's kind,
But I think he lacks
An intelligent mind.

He slobbers and drools
All over the place,
Sniffs my wet feet
And kisses my face.

My little dog Bullet
Has a banged up head,
It's bruised black and blue
With a spot crimson red.

I wish he could talk
Cause I don't have a clue,
How he got that bump
That's all black and blue.

He ran out of the house
Though his body was frail,
But like a good spy
I was hot on his trail.

I just had to know
What happened today,
So I hid by a tree
Some distance away.

He ran wild and crazy
He was sweaty and hot,
Then the mystery unfolded
Right there on the spot.

Oh, now I see why
He is bruised up and marked,
He's been chasing the cars
That our neighbors had parked.

A more wonderful dog
You never would find,
Now I'm certain he lacks
An intelligent mind.

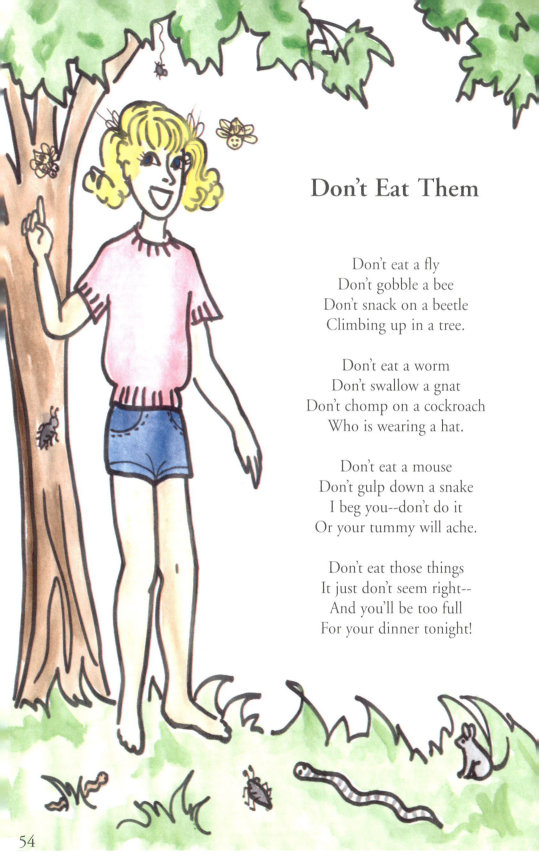

Don't Eat Them

Don't eat a fly
Don't gobble a bee
Don't snack on a beetle
Climbing up in a tree.

Don't eat a worm
Don't swallow a gnat
Don't chomp on a cockroach
Who is wearing a hat.

Don't eat a mouse
Don't gulp down a snake
I beg you--don't do it
Or your tummy will ache.

Don't eat those things
It just don't seem right--
And you'll be too full
For your dinner tonight!

If

If the ocean had a hole in it's floor
  And the water drained all out,
  We'd be drinking lots of milk
  And getting strong no doubt.

If the ocean had a hole in it's floor
  What treasures would we find?
  A sunken ship, some emeralds
  Or mysteries of mankind?

If the ocean had a hole in it's floor
  How could the fish survive?
  Would the seaweed all dry up
  And might anyone be alive?

That small word "if" sure bothers me
  And would be a huge disaster--
So if that happened I'd patch the hole
  With milk and concrete plaster.

Play Ball

I can hear the fans cheering
It's a hot humid day.
I don't like this game
But I'll play anyway.

Bart slid into second base
Jason got to third.
Macho Louie muscled up
And coach said not a word.

George O'Dell slid into home
Blood came oozing out.
He just smiled and strutted off
He loved the game no doubt.

I really couldn't concentrate
The sun glared in my eyes.
I got up and hit the ball
Much to everyone's surprise.

I wonder why my teammates
think this baseball game is fun.
I'm going to the outfield--
When will this game be done?

My heart just isn't in this game
But I'll be tough somehow--
Cause dad said it will do me good
It's a fly ball, HOLY COW!

"That's okay." I heard dad yell
With his hand cupped to his face.
"Everybody messes up
So you are no disgrace."

I looked at coach, a robust man
And saw the mental strain.
He mumbled underneath his breath
And I knew he was in pain.

The score is tied up six to six
And the best I can recall--
It seems like twenty minutes
Since I have touched the ball.

Look, the crowd is leaving
The game has gotten over.
I guess I didn't notice--
I was busy picking clover!

Lonliest Birthday Party

I had a birthday party
Not a single person came.
I danced around the living room
Then played a party game.

Blew out all my candles
Ate a giant piece of cake.
Threw some colorful confetti
Then got a bellyache.

Sang happy birthday to myself
And it was quite a scream,
Celebrating all alone
Then scooping up ice cream.

There wasn't any presents
Stacked up on the floor,
But I just kept on listening
For a knock on my front door.

My party sure was lonely
For I had high expectations--
So next year I'll remember
To mail out the invitations!

Quilts Of Many Colors

Everyday at half past eight
Her sewing machine would soar,
And when she got some squares cut out
The pedal would hit the floor.

As each new quilt was finished
She'd stack them very neat,
Then sew just like a maniac
With magic hands and feet.

There were quilts of many colors
They had a lot of flair.
Some baby quilts and camping quilts
Were piled next to her chair.

She kept stacking all those quilts
Til they were nine feet high,
Then she spied a raveled thread
From the corner of her eye.

Her son came by to visit
But only saw her hair.
He couldn't find the rest of her
In that pile beside the chair.

She moaned out loud so he would hear
Then shouted, "Get some stilts!
I'm way up here next to the light
Stuck **on top of all these quilts!**"

Foul Mood

I'm in a foul mood
I'm mad as can be
Stay out of my room
And don't talk to me.

I'm in a foul mood
I just kicked my bed
Threw a big tantrum
Now my face is all red.

I'm in a foul mood
I've got nothing to say
So don't talk me out
Of this foul mood today.

I'm in a foul mood
And mad as the dickens
So I'll head for the coop
And move in with the chickens.

Decisions Decisions

Sweet young Melissa got up one day
To go for a little bike ride.
She tried to pick out a really cool dress
But Melissa just couldn't decide.

Sweet young Melissa thought to herself
I want to look pretty and sweet.
It's such a fine day with Spring in the air
Who knows what boy I shall meet.

Shall I wear pink or shall I wear green
Or how 'bout some ruffles of blue?
This polka dot dress looks pretty cute
Or maybe this brown one will do.

Poor young Melissa was in a big jam
With her dresses piled high in the air.
She couldn't decide which one to pick
And her closet was totally bare.

She spent the whole day racking her brain
It made a big mess of her head.
The sun had come up but quickly was gone,
So Melissa just went back to bed.

Crispy Done

Got a sunburn on my nose,
On my arms and on my toes.
Got it on my back and head
It hurt so bad I went to bed.

Got a sunburn in my eyes,
On my legs and on my thighs.
In my nostril's, in my ears
I've cried and cried a hundred tears.

I'm very red just like a beet,
Crispy done from head to feet.
It hurts a lot to blink my eye
To laugh or even make a sigh.

Look at me! My sunburns gone
Now I can get my swimsuit on,
So don't call me to come and play--
I'm headed for the beach today!

A Geep

If you ever see a geep
Don't breathe a sigh or make a peep,
Cause if you make one bit of noise
He will trip on all your toys.

If you ever see a geep
Don't let him drive your mama's jeep,
Cause he's a nut behind the wheel
And loves to make the rubber squeal.

If you ever see a geep
Don't sail across the ocean deep,
For he's the captain of the boat
Don't sail with him you may not float.

If you ever see a geep
Don't hide your eyes and start to weep,
Because he's harmless as can be
And visits you at half past three.

Have you? Have you seen a geep?
I bet you've seen him in your sleep,
When you ate lots of salty food
Or you were in a crabby mood.

Now have you ever seen a geep
With fifteen arms piled in a heap?
His snaggle teeth all bloody red
And nine small eyeballs in his head.

If you ever see a geep
Don't judge and say he is a creep,
Because those arms piled in a heap
Will protect you nicely while you sleep.

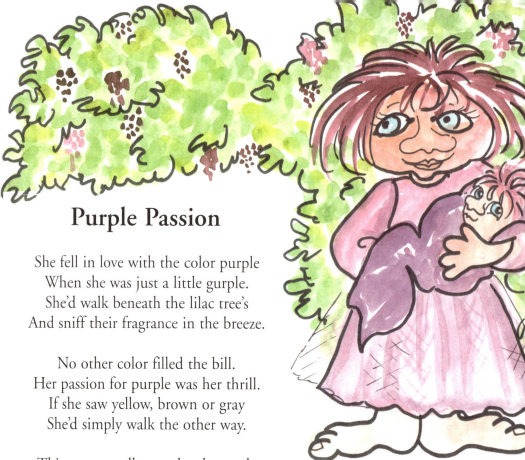

Purple Passion

She fell in love with the color purple
When she was just a little gurple.
She'd walk beneath the lilac tree's
And sniff their fragrance in the breeze.

No other color filled the bill.
Her passion for purple was her thrill.
If she saw yellow, brown or gray
She'd simply walk the other way.

This young troll was a lovely gurple
And soon she married Mr. Purple.
They had a troll and you can bet
Was rightly named sweet Violet.

Purple pillows, purple dishes
Lots of tiny purple fishes.
Purple ribbons, purple bows
And purple kleenex for her nose.

One day her little Violet wed
To her sweetie named Mr. Red.
Her mother adored sweet Violet
But she just had one small regret.

She wished that Mr. Red was purple.
That troll who married her little gurple.
He really seemed quite nice enough
But he lacked all the purple stuff.

Quickly passed the hours and days
As others watched his kindly ways.
Folks loved that troll named Mr. Red
With only good thoughts in his head.

He treated Violet like a queen.
They loved the colors of pink and green.
A nicer couple you'd never see
As they bounced a sweet troll on their knee.

The mother of sweet Violet dear
Changed her views and shed a tear.
Now she's become a lot more wise
As she sees the world through Violet's eyes.

Moody Mark

"I'm running away," said mad moody Mark.
"I'm going to sleep at the town's city park.

I can't watch TV past the hour of ten,
And my skimpy allowance gets missed now and then.

I cannot eat cookies or cake when I like,
And my spoiled brother keeps riding my bike.

I'm running away now don't hold me back.
Soon I will be eating from a brown paper sack."

My mother came in and hugged me goodbye.
Dad said, "Later dude!" as he swatted a fly.

Soon he was off snoring in his favorite chair,
And my sister Lucy was curling her hair.

Gosh, I think I'll stay here it's been a hard day--
They took all the fun out of running away!

Gobbledy Goop

Jibberty jabberty, gobbledy goop--
She's coming over to make you some soup.

She'll ride on a broom with her kettle and cat
Wearing a cape and a ragged old hat.

Her teeth are all yellow, there's a wart on her nose
And it has been said she's got wrinkly toes.

Jibberty jabberty, gobbledy goop--
She will prepare you a hot tasty soup.

She'll boil a possum, a frog and a lizzard
Then saute' nicely a big piece of gizzard.

She'll toss in a spider, a crocodile's eye
And three pickled pig's feet that were hung out to dry.

The table's been set but don't be afraid--
This soup will taste better than your Aunt Bertha made!

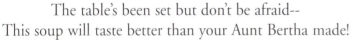

In-Between

I'm the cheese between two crackers.
The ham between some bread.
The one between some flannel sheets
Inside a warm soft bed.

The tongue between some crooked teeth.
Cement between some bricks.
In the barnyard I'm the hen
Between two baby chicks.

A book between some bookends.
A nose between some eyes.
The bird that's flying fancy free
In-between the earth and skies.

I really didn't ask to be
Stuck always "in-between"
Little blonde haired Betty Ann
And blue eyed Mary Jean.

No, I couldn't pick my order
In our all girl family tree,
But I am glad I'm "in-between"
Number one and number three.

When I am feeling comical
Like a harp between two horns,
I smile and say, "I'm like a rose
Stuck in-between two thorns!"

Rainstorm

Look out, it's raining dogs and cats
It's pouring lizzards and black bats.

Oh my, it's raining squawking parrots
And rabbits who are eating carrots.

Good grief, it's raining pots and pans
And rusted chicken noodle cans.

Look out, it's raining old black wigs
It's raining three new baby pigs.

The rain has stopped and was a dandy--
But why, oh why, couldn't it rain candy?

Mean Selfish Guy

Don't touch that it's mine!
Don't touch it I swear!
I really love chocolate
And I don't want to share.

This single dipped cone
Is real creamy and sweet,
And it tastes really yummy
Way down to my feet.

Mmm--my best friend came out
With a humongous cone.
I'll sit here beside him
Cause he looks all alone.

He's got five giant scoops
Compared to my one,
And it looks scrumdelicious
Cause mine is all done.

"Do you mind if I nibble
With this small plastic spoon?"
He snapped, "Get your own
And take a hike to the moon."

Boy, he's sure acting stingy
With that gleam in his eye.
I wonder what gives--
With that mean selfish guy!

Make Believe Brother

If I had a brother--he'd be like no other
I know he'd be gentle and strong.
When he would go out I haven't a doubt
He would take his cute sister along.

If I had a brother--he'd be like no other
He would willingly take out the trash.
He'd always say, "hi" with a sweet loving sigh
And lend me some much needed cash.

If I had a brother--he'd be like no other
He'd surely not tattle or cry.
When he had a choice, I would rightly rejoice
As he gave me the big piece of pie.

If I had a brother--he'd be like no other
He would always take care of the cat.
Heck, I'm out of my mind to think I would find
A big brother who acted like that!

A To G

We loaded up our yellow car
Piled high with pop and food.
I was really quite excited
And in a darn good mood.

Grandpa said, "Let's find some peace."
We snuggled side by side.
There were seven of us boys
And we were daddy's pride.

We were named from A to G.
I was the youngest one.
They named me "George" and mother said,
That she was overdone!

Dad worked very hard each day
So it occured to me,
He needed a vacation
With his boys from A to G.

We pitched our tent beneath the stars
Ate hot dogs on a stick,
Roasted eighty-four marshmallow's
And not one of us got sick.

"I'm going for a walk," I said,
"But I'll take brother 'Bill'."
We trekked off and waved goodbye,
Then scampered up the hill.

I started looking high and low
For we only had a while,
And then before I knew it
We'd walked a country mile.

I looked inside the water
Searched high up in the tree's,
Overturned a hundred rocks
And scraped up both my knee's.

It wasn't out there anywhere
So we headed down the bank,
Then noticed from a distance
My dad and brother "Frank".

They saw my disappointment
As my poor head hung low,
I said, "I couldn't find it,"
And out the tears did flow.

"Grandpa told us find some peace
And there's no wiser man.
I tried my best to find it,"
Then my father smiled with "Dan".

"Al" and "Calvin" scooped me up
along with brother "Ed",
Then I knew what "peace" he meant
And not a word was said.

So if you're looking for some peace
Don't search high in a tree.
Look inside your family circle
With your brothers A to G.

Melvina's Trip To The Store

They sent Melvina to the store
She bought a squeaky rusted door.

She chose some slippers for her feet
Then got a purple toilet seat.

Picked a toothy crocodile
Stacked twenty books up in a pile.

Found a loud mischievous ape
And clothed him in a long red cape.

Bought a lantern and a pear
Threw in some ribbons for her hair.

Got a hammer and a coat
Added one white billy goat.

When she was finally set to go
She grabbed some band-aids for her toe.

Melvina had a lovely time
But she was broke without a dime.

Then she moaned a great big sigh
"Now what was I supposed to buy?"

Do Not Tell A Lie

Do not tell a lie
Because if you do,
Your nose will sprout mushrooms
And your face will turn blue.

Your eyes will bulge out,
Your teeth will decay,
And most of your friends
Will run far away.

Your tongue will curl up
And get horribly red,
Then green slimy worms
Will camp on your head.

If you tell a lie
Mold will grow on your feet,
And people will scream
When you walk down the street.

Please don't tell a lie
Because it's not cool,
And people who lie
Look like a big fool.

Oh, I must be leaving
I am suddenly blue,
And to be very honest
I lied to you.

So I'll hang my head
With shame I suppose--
And go scrape these mushrooms
Right off of my nose.

When Preston Ate Bugs

Preston ate a slimy worm
And I let out a giggle,
But as it dangled in his throat
It made a desperate wiggle!

Next he ate a hairy fly
Chewed it up like tender meat.
He said, " This sure tastes yummy
Quite delectable and sweet."

He was always showing off
To kids and older folks,
Pretending he was eating bugs
Or telling crazy jokes.

We invited him to dinner
Like we did on any day,
But when the lid came off the pan
He fainted dead away.

He woke up, turned dark green
Went running down the street,
Acting like a maniac
With tangled size ten feet.

We hollered, "What is wrong with you?"
Then we saw his poor legs quiver,
He moaned but didn't once look back
"Ughh--how CAN you eat that liver?"

School Daze

We rode the yellow school bus
I yanked her pony tail.
She turned around and slugged me
And I let out a wail.

I chased her through the school yard
She kicked my spelling book.
I stuck my tongue out really big
And she gave me a dirty look.

She told me I had cooties
I said, "Here's one to eat."
She said, "You really gross me out,"
Then she chased me down the street.

I never saw that girl again
But I'm sure without a doubt,
I'll never forget that pretty girl
I was so wild about.

77

Grandpa's Throat

I heard grandpa tell my dad
"I think it's gonna rain,
Cause down inside my little toe
I've got an aching pain.

My back ain't what it used to be
I feel like an old goat,
And I am really quite annoyed
With this frog that's in my throat."

Grandpa went to take a nap
So I acted really quick.
I grabbed my yellow flashlight
Hoping it would do the trick.

In his mouth with a steady hand
I shined my light inside.
Sure glad that he was fast asleep
Or he would have my hide.

It looks really weird in here
It's deep and dark and cold,
But there's some really nifty stuff--
I think I see green mold.

I think I've found some seaweed
And a lobster tail that's pink.
Is this a mini hair ball?
It's tame, I hope, I think.

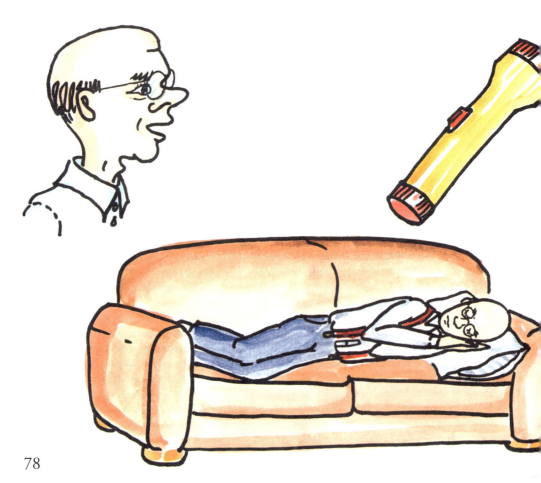

Here's a slimy wet banana peel
And a leprechaun in red.
Hey, dig these crazy glasses
Grandpa wore upon his head.

A bunch of dancing ladies
And a black and white TV.
A toy soldier standing tall
With a band-aid on his knee.

Pink gobs of gum, a violin
A purple submarine.
This really was the coolest stuff
That I had ever seen.

I was really, really frantic
And in desperate despair,
And long before I knew it
Grandpa's stuff was everywhere.

I couldn't believe it wasn't there
Had my searching been in vain?
I couldn't find it anywhere--
Look out, here comes a train.

There's nothing left in grandpa's mouth
So I'll end upon this note,
Cause I found everything on earth
But the frog in grandpa's throat.

79

Queen Bee & The Fly

They had a love-**flea** wedding
For a **queen bee** and a **fly**.
She wore a honey-colored dress
He gave a loving sigh.

She whispered, "I'll **bee** true to you."
He said, "Come **fly** with me."
They gazed into each others eyes
Then drank some sugared tea.

Gnat Keen Coal came buzzing in
and sang a tender song.
He mingled with the others
But didn't stay too long.

All their friends were chatting
With **Ant** Agnus and her crowd,
Then someone said, "Let's **flea** from here
This band is way too loud."

Yes, everyone was all **tick**ed off
Because the band was loud,
But the **queen bee** and her honey
Didn't seem to need a crowd.

So if you have a wedding
On a love-**flea** day in June,
Those **tick**ed off guests won't **bug** you
Cause you'll **bee** on your honeymoon.

Monster's Manicure

A monster and her girlfriend
Stopped by the beauty school,
To get a little manicure
So they'd look really cool.

They giggled like two school girls
As they squeezed into their seat,
Scarfed down thirteen candy bars
For an extra little treat.

There were lots of pretty colors
But both chose "peachy pink",
So a great big fight erupted
And they landed in the sink.

Stuff was flying left and right
As they pulled each other's hair.
The walls got really splattered
And they broke a wooden chair.

The room got eerie silent
And when the brawl was done,
One gal quipped, "Let's come next week
I have NEVER had more fun."

A Huge Fish Story

He darted out in front of me
I saw his two eyes glare.
He opened up his big ole mouth
And gave me quite a scare.

He was really frightening
And had a nasty bark.
I wasn't very comfortable
With that gigantic shark.

A slimy eel came swimming by
And I really had a hunch,
He was looking weird at me
With idea's for his lunch.

Some brightly colored goldfish
A huge ten-legged squid,
Were really overwhelming
Because I was a kid.

I glanced over to my left
And from a coral reef,
A crab with two long pincers
Was close to me, good grief!

A soft eight-legged octopus
Didn't have much charm.
He was seven feet from me
With suckers on each arm.

I was totally surrounded
As they came to make their call,
And I'm sure I must have counted
Two thousand fish in all.

Those creatures sure were scary
As they hovered in the sea,
But I am glad the aquarium glass
Was between the fish and me!

Grandpa Harris

Dear Grandpa Harris flew out to Paris
To climb the Eiffel Tower.
Lathered up in the rain on a street in Spain
And took a much needed shower.

Rode a toboggon and cracked his poor noggin
While yodeling high in the alps.
Went to Botswana and ate an iguana.
Met some Pygmies who were hunting for scalps.

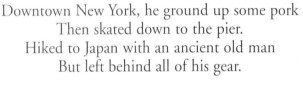

Went back to Spain on a rickety train
That broke down six times or more.
Sailed a boat to Peru and went straight to the zoo
To nap on the elephant's floor.

Downtown New York, he ground up some pork
Then skated down to the pier.
Hiked to Japan with an ancient old man
But left behind all of his gear.

Dear Grandpa Harris didn't mean to embarrass
For he was good hearted and kind.
He traveled those places and saw all those faces,
But only in his mind!

Elephant's Trunk

Have you ever stopped and wondered
Why an elephant has a trunk?
Is he packing for vacation
And filling it with junk?

Does he have a giant toothbrush
A towel, a shirt and comb?
Will he be traveling far away
Or be hanging out at home?

I'm sure that gray ole elephant
Really does not care,
If he has four new sneakers
Or thirty strands of hair.

I'll bet he doesn't give a hoot
On any given day,
If anybody wanders by
While he gobbles up his hay.

I'll drop this quest about his trunk
But one thing bothers me,
If it really is a trunk
Then where the heck's the key?

Wrinkly Old Pickles

We brought a jar of pickles home
And set them by the sink,
But I did not imagine
That I saw those pickles blink.

There were skinny ones and fat ones
And some of them looked old.
I checked the pickles out again
But they made my blood run cold.

These pickles look quite eerie
All squished here side by side,
So I'll just take another peek
Then find a place to hide.

I'm nervous and I'm all freaked out
From those pickles watching me,
But I'm still very curious
If those warty eyes can see.

I'm off to buy a burger now
With lots of cheddar cheese,
But one thing I'll insist upon
Is hold the pickles please!

Spoiled & Demanding

She's lazy and she's arrogant
She's got an attitude,
And she is really picky
About her choice of food.

Often she'll play ball with me
But sometimes not at all.
She ignores the whole darn family
As she prances down the hall.

All she does is sleep all day
Then wakes and gives a yawn,
She always tries to run away
When we put her sweater on.

Yes, she's spoiled and demanding
Now what do you think of that?
I wonder what I'd ever do
Without my precious cat!

The Grand Buffet

We went to the grand buffet
Last Tuesday night at eight.
My brother Paul cut through the line
Because he couldn't wait.

He got a fork, grabbed his plate
Then piled it way up high,
With roast beef and potatoes
And boston chocolate pie.

Three helpings of spaghetti
Some tuna casserole,
Linguini and a taco
And Cajun shrimp creole.

Some lobster tails, green jello
And twelve big slabs of pork,
Were hanging off my brothers plate
And he wouldn't use his fork.

His mouth was smeared with ketsup
There at the grand buffet,
And when he belched a giant one
My family looked away.

Now all that seemed irrelevant
As he performed his show,
But mother fainted when he said
"I'll have a plate to go!"

The Mule

I hauled sister on my back
All the way to Lincoln School.
She wasn't very heavy
So I packed her like a mule.

We would stop and rest a bit
And shiver from the cold.
She was just a youngster
But I was ten years old.

I hauled sister on my back
She was the "clinging" kind,
But if a person so inquired
I really didn't mind.

I hauled sister on my back
And much to our surprise,
We slowly made it to the school
While dirt blew in our eyes.

I think I was half stupid
Or had loose screws I fear,
But I just couldn't stand the sight
Of a little sister's tear.

I hauled sister on my back
So when I'm eighty-three,
I'll ask her with a sheepish grin
"Hey Sis--will you carry me?"

Pryin' Me Open

My doctor said, "Stick out your tongue!"
So I pressed my lips real tight,
And shook my head in protest
While my doctor's face turned white.

He tried to pry me open
With a little wooden stick,
Put a feather up my nose
But that didn't do the trick.

Next thing I knew he tried a wrench
But I didn't even budge,
So he tempted me with brownies
Topped with thick and gooey fudge.

He brought a green bulldozer in
But it missed me by an inch,
Sent eighteen pretty nurses by
But I didn't even flinch.

That room was a big disaster
Dust was flying everywhere,
And everybody next to me
Had dirt stuck in their hair.

I finally opened up my mouth
To breathe a great big sigh,
My doctor stood beside me
And looked me in the eye.

He said again, "Stick out your tongue!"
I felt his dismal mood,
But I said matter of factly
"My mother says it's rude!"

Snuffle Hill

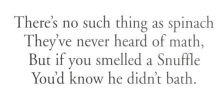

Have you ever been to Snuffle Hill?
Come on, now if you dare,
Jump on my magic carpet
And I will take us there.

I've been told on Snuffle Hill
They never comb their hair,
They never ever brush their teeth
Or change their underwear.

There's no such thing as spinach
They've never heard of math,
But if you smelled a Snuffle
You'd know he didn't bath.

Snuffle Hill is up ahead
The lights are all aglow,
Big flies are hovering around
Each place the Snuffle's go.

There's smelly trash and soiled clothes
Thrown in a giant hump,
And I'm not feeling very well
Cause it smells like a dump.

Hang on, I think we'll turn around
And choose another path,
But rest assured when I get home
I'll be glad to take a bath!

Marshmallow Dream

I ate some spicy meatballs
Before I went to bed.
I had a really crazy dream
With weird stuff in my head.

I dreamed about a monster
Driving in a car,
Then he was swimming frantically
In a tub of gooey tar.

Up and down the street I ran
In my jammies and a hat.
Next thing I knew I had six arms
And I was up to bat.

Some tree's were falling over
With monkey's everywhere,
And angels in the heaven
Were braiding up their hair.

I was fearlessly sky diving
In a silky dress of pink,
And snakes were chatting happily
Inside our kitchen sink.

A fluffy white marshmallow
Was brought for me to eat.
It tasted rather gummy
But wasn't very sweet.

I'm suddenly awakened now
Yuk, what's this bitter taste?
There's feathers in-between my teeth
mixed in with sticky paste.

My stomach's fat and bloated
And I really do feel weird.
I cannot find my pillow--
It has strangely disappeared!

The Viper

The viper is coming
He's got three scaly toes.
There's a horn on his head
And he's got a red nose.

The viper is coming
He's sneezin' and wheezin',
And he's really quite sick
Of this allergy season.

The viper is here
The folks ran away.
All the little kids hid
Behind a pile of hay.

The viper is chatting
With a big orange ox.
He's holding some kleenex
In a bright colored box.

Don't be scared of the viper
With his three scaly toes,
Cause he will be leaving
when he "vipes" his red nose.

Teeny Tiny Seed

Once I found a tiny seed
I stuck it in the ground.
I watered it both day and night
And watched it like a hound.

Every day it grew and grew
Til it was ten feet high.
It was pretty awesome
As it reached towards the sky.

A news reporter talked to me
And wrote a lengthy story.
My photograph was everywhere
And I was in my glory.

Crowds of people all came by
And trampled down our lawn.
They were yelling loudly
Each day from dusk til dawn.

Our town was in an uproar
The mayor took a stand.
They took an axe to my poor tree
And it plunked down in the sand.

Things got back to normal
And no one noticed me.
Soon everyone forgot about
My giant ten foot tree.

Spring is in the air again
Look, I've found another seed!
There's only one place it belongs
In the garbage can INDEED!

93

That Stupid Yo-Yo

He stood there on the blacktop
With a yo-yo in his hand,
And all the young girls at his school
Thought he was something grand.

His hands were just like magic
And that yo-yo of bright red,
Kept on going up and down
But he didn't move his head.

He was short and pudgy
And cute as he could be,
But I was always wondering
If he'd ever notice me.

Every time I saw him
Come wind or snow or sleet,
He'd tug upon my heart string
And make it skip a beat.

He didn't bat an eyelash
Cause he loved his yo-yo game.
Each day I watched him closely
And of course I knew his name.

I'd run by and scream out loud
So that pudgy boy would see,
That I was wild about him
But he didn't look at me.

All my efforts were in vain
And I thought how could this be?
That he chose that stupid yo-yo
Instead of choosing me!

Just Be Nice

Be nice to Aunt Fran who lives in Spokane.
Be nice to your weird neighbor Fred.
Be nice to Miss Jane who's slightly insane
With a bird nest on top of her head.

Be nice to a witch who sleeps in a ditch.
Be nice to a bald-headed bear.
Be nice to a swami who eats moldy salami
Then sits upside down in his chair.

Be nice to a snake with a bad bellyache.
Be nice to old Doctor Jones.
Be nice if you can to head hunter Dan
Who has a collection of bones.

Now take my advice and be very nice
To your dad who seldom is funny.
Be nice day and night and don't pick a fight,
Because he's got all of the MONEY!

Eight Foot Arms

I wish my arms were eight feet tall
Then I'd be great at basketball.
I'd score a hundred points at least
Acting like a wild beast.

Eight foot arms would look real cool
And I'd be famous at my school.
Though I would look a bit off key
At least the girls would notice me.

If eight foot arms were really mine
I'd keep the bullies all in line,
Then later if they came to call
I'd pin them up against the wall.

Eight foot arms I wish--but wait
I don't want them stuck in the gate.
They'd be real hard to drag around
And I couldn't keep them off the ground.

I'd have a sore on my poor thumb
And my fingers would step in bubble gum.
I'll keep my old arms they're not bad.
They're the greatest arms I ever had.

Closet Menagerie

I cleaned out my closet
One dark cloudy day
Because it was raining
And I couldn't play.

Found a neat shiny marble
A bubble gum card
A gray and white pebble
That came from my yard.

I found a wet shoe
And a sock with no mate
A dried squiggly worm
I used once for bait.

Twelve comics, eight puzzles
Some green gooey slime
A broken down watch
That wouldn't tell time.

A box filled with seashells
A black rubber bug
My frisbee, my slingshot
A Chicago Bears mug.

Now my stuff's in a pile
Way up to the sky
And I love all this mess
Though I can't explain why.

But one thing's for sure--
It's worth you can't measure
Cause all of this "junk"
Is a little kid's treasure.

Brilliant Beth

Shhh--brilliant Beth is hard at work
She's searching for a cure,
For rare unknown diseases
So please don't bother her.

A microscope is always close
She looks at lots of germs,
She'll open up a big glass jar
Then dissect lots of worms.

Her nose is to the grindstone
Her feet are on the ground,
And while she's testing moldy things
She never makes a sound.

Shhh--brilliant Beth is hard at work
But I just heard startling news--
Though she's a real Einstein
She cannot tie her shoes!

The Thinkin' Rock

I climbed up a big ole hill
And there I found my Uncle Will.
He was sitting on a rock
And shushed me when I tried to talk.

This rock here is the thinkin' rock
Please sit still and do not talk.
I sat and watched that rock all day
When it got dark I went away.

Next day I climbed up to the hill
To be with good ole Uncle Will.
I gawked around and watched a bee
And felt red ants crawl up on me.

I watched that rock from nine til four
But couldn't watch it anymore.
My eyes were red, my mouth was dry
So I bid Uncle Will goodbye.

I never more climbed up that hill
Cause I was ticked at Uncle Will.
And you can bet I raised a stink
Cause I never once saw that rock think!

The Gentle Goldminer

There was a goldminer
Who lived in the hills.
He lived in a shack
With no fancies or frills.

People would come
From miles away.
All kinds of people
Would come every day.

Some folks would ask
And be rather bold,
"Do you have any nuggets
That are made of pure gold?"

If it was raining
Or storming out there,
The "fifty cent" tour
Was still given with care.

Now some of those people
Would plot selfishly,
And think to themselves
"What's in this for me?"

That goldminer fella'
Was such a nice guy,
But most people wanted
A piece of the pie.

One day the gold mine
Went as dry as could be,
And you're right if you guessed
NO MORE COMPANY!

Scummy Teeth

I didn't brush my scummy teeth
For three days in a row,
Because I figured what the heck--
No one would ever know.

I always slept in way too late
My life was disarray,
But everything was different
There at my school today.

I smiled a big wide toothy grin
The kids all ran away,
My teacher found a corner
And didn't move all day.

The janitor finally told me
Right there on the spot,
My teeth looked really gnarly
And my breath was not so hot.

There was tuna fish and carrots
Black raisins stuck there too,
Some eggs I had for breakfast
And part of last night's stew.

They're acting like I've got the plague
But I'll shed no tears of sorrow,
Because I'll have an instant lunch
When I'm at school tomorrow.

Camp

My folks sent me to camp one year
And didn't even shed a tear.
I really thought they both would cry
When I waved and said goodbye.

They said, "Now rest and have some fun,
Do some things you haven't done.
We think it will be good for you--
You'll be refreshed and feel like new."

At five a.m. they blew the horn
That woke us loudly every morn.
We hiked, then rowed a big canoe
Then hiked again when we got through.

Climbed a mountain, cooked some stew
Lost my orange tennis shoe,
Formed an awesome relay team
And sipped our water from a stream.

Sang some songs around the fire
Cut my knee on old barbed wire,
Had a dance and gazed at stars
Stayed up all night to capture Mars.

Ran some races, climbed a rope
Slipped on someone's bar of soap,
Mosquitos bit me--so did the ants
Some crawled up inside my pants.

I'm going home, I'm tuckered out
I'm all worn out without a doubt.
It's weird, I sure don't feel my best--
I'll have to go back home to rest!

Cool Average Joe

My sister's boyfriend came to call
To take her on a date.
He was spruced up in fine leather
And my sister couldn't wait.

He hopped out of his black car
And stepped on Fido's toe.
He didn't look unusual
Just like an average Joe.

He tripped on mother's flower pot
And badly bruised his leg.
Hit his head beneath our elm tree
And got a big goose egg.

Joe sat inside the living room
My mother served him pie.
I edged a wee bit closer
And looked him in the eye.

He was pretty cool and casual
And I liked the way he talked,
But I couldn't even get a peek
Til he got up to walk.

My sister made her entrance
And said, "I'm ready Joe."
He stood up and I did too
As they prepared to go.

I didn't want to stare too long
As he got up from his seat,
But someone told me yesterday
That Joe had two left feet!

Silly Sally

Silly Sally made a cake
Standing on one leg.
She tossed a squawking chicken in
When the book said add one egg.

Ten cups of grease were measured
With lots of garlic too.
She added chopped up broccoli
Some toe nails and a shoe.

She cut a slab of liver up
Because she loved the taste.
Tossed in a head of cabbage
And a can of gooey paste.

She beat it with the mixer
And baked it in the sun,
Then stuck it with a pitchfork
To see if it was done.

Silly Sally you are strange
And your cake is weird indeed,
But why did you lick the beaters
With the mixer on high speed?

A Big Hunch

I have a big hunch they eat humans for lunch
And will simmer us in a big pot,
With garlic and onions on top of our heads
And served up as soon as we're hot.

I have a big hunch they will spice up their lunch
With ketsup and mustard and sauce--
And when they are finished I really doubt
They will take five minutes to floss.

I have a big hunch it will be a gross lunch
With our eyeballs and hair all agoop.
Some slimy green seaweed and vinegar too
Will make it a really weird soup.

I have a big hunch they were ready for lunch
But they all got into a fight,
About how much pepper to use on our heads
And if they could sample a bite.

I have a big hunch they won't get us for lunch
Cause the pot is tipped over in rage.
So long, see ya later--I have a big hunch
I'll be running fast off of this page!

Awkward

He spilled a milkshake on her dress
It made a really sloppy mess.

She smiled at him, he couldn't speak
His tongue was tied, his knee's were weak.

They ordered burgers and some fries
He gazed into her deep brown eyes.

He squeezed the ketsup, it went splatter
She acted like it didn't matter.

He felt just like a stupid goat
When he got mixed up and wore her coat.

They walked home and hugged goodnight--
She said, "This date has been just right."

I guess things really weren't that bad
The night my mother met my dad.

Mom's Lilac Tree

I think that I shall never see
Another pretty lilac tree.
One that smelled so perfume sweet,
The nicest tree on our whole street.

I think that I shall never see
Another lovely lilac tree.
One whose leaves were bright and green,
The biggest tree you ever seen.

I think that I don't want to see
My angry mom who's sore with me,
Cause my cool axe I got from town
ACCIDENTLY chopped her nice tree down.

I'm sure that I will never see
One thin dime or one penny,
Until that tree is paid in full
Heck, I don't think my axe is cool!

Flora McNubble

Flora McNubble was always in trouble
Because her manners were bad.
She'd yell at one brother then hit the other.
What a terrible temper she had.

Flora McNubble was always in trouble
At dinner she'd make a huge mess.
She'd spit out her food when it was all chewed,
Then wipe off her mouth with her dress.

She'd belch a big burp and make a loud slurp
Put carrots inside of her nose.
Scarf down her hot stew in one gulp or two,
Then eat with all ten of her toes.

She'd squish her spaghetti to look like confetti
Then splat it all over the door.
When she was all through her face would turn blue,
Then she'd get down and lick up the floor.

Flora McNubble you are quite a good double
For a piggy who slurps from a pail.
Oh my goodness me--what is this I see?
You have grown a curly pink tail.

Johnny McGrue

Young Johnny McGrue
Was an odd sort of kid.
Didn't do all the things
The other boys did.

He didn't play football
And he didn't swim,
So all of the kids
Looked oddly at him.

His curly brown hair
Wasn't combed very neat,
And more times than not
He'd trip over his feet.

Yes, Johnny McGrue
Was an odd sort of chap,
And when he would smile
His teeth showed a gap.

Most days he'd stay home
And play with his brother,
Read a good book
Or chat with his mother.

Some people would snicker
And whisper, "He's odd--"
Then walk slowly away
With a pitiful nod.

It seems we're ALL odd
Like Johnny McGrue,
But if odd were defined
We'd compare it to who?

The Hairy Tooth Fairy

I sat on my bed
With the nice tooth fairy.
She was squatty and short
And really quite hairy.

Her big eyes poked out
On the side of her head,
And I giggled out loud
Cause her name was Fred.

She opened her mouth
And back underneath,
Her tonsils were orange
Just like her teeth.

She was real homely
And not ordinary.
She was squatty and short
And really quite hairy.

Her socks didn't match
She was haggered and old,
And quite honestly she
was a sight to behold.

I'm sure I'd not seen
This kind of a fairy,
And oh, did I mention
She was really quite hairy?

Her strange magic wand
Was a skinny black stick,
And she told me bluntly
It would still do the trick.

I told her I thought
That black stick wouldn't do,
So I argued with her
Til I was dark blue.

Then poof, she was gone
Right out of my sight,
And I searched for her
Long into the night.

Next time I won't argue
Cause I don't think it's funny,
That the tooth fairy vanished
And left me no money.

Poor Poor Lenny

I stopped by cousin Lenny's house
To hang out for a while,
But when my aunt came to the door
She didn't crack a smile.

Tears were streaming down her cheeks
And she was in despair.
I asked if Lenny was at home.
She said he wasn't there.

She said, "He's at the hospital
Don't know when he'll be back."
I hopped fast like a rabbit
To tell our buddy Jack.

We ran down to the flower shop
As we wiped our tears away.
We carried all the money
We'd saved up since last May.

We got inside the hospital
And couldn't believe our eyes.
There stood Lenny and Uncle Bill
And it took us by surprise.

They had come to see a friend
And Lenny wasn't ill,
But everything worked out that day
Thanks to Uncle Bill.

He bought us fries and burgers
Some pizza and a shake,
Then took us to a ballgame
And bought us chocolate cake.

Then he bought our rose bouguet
And gave it to his friend.
We got every single penny back
And made out in the end.

I told him about Aunt Cora's tears
Then came his quick reply--
"She was chopping onions up
That's what made her cry."

Lester Lumplefink

Little Lester Lumplefink
Didn't like the color pink.
He said, "It's just for sissy boys
And it looks stupid on my toys."

Pink ice-cream he wouldn't lick
Wouldn't eat pink candy on a stick.
If he passed a sweet pink rose
He'd blast it with a garden hose.

His sister wore pink shoes to work
And when she did--he went berserk.
A knitted quilt of pink with lace
Made him distort and twist his face.

Little Lester Lumplefink
You are standing by some pink.
You're staring at that pretty gal
Next to your favorite cousin Hal.

She's all dressed up from head to toe
In a cute pink dress with matching bow.
There's a dimple on her chin
And you have got a cheesy grin.

Lester, can you hear me call?
You haven't moved your head at all.
"Shhh," he said without a blink.
"I'm in love with the color pink."

My Awful Cold

My nose was running down my mouth
I couldn't make it stop.
I needed rest and medicine
But I wanted soda pop.

I sniffed and coughed the whole day long
My nose ran everywhere.
I was bored inside in my bed
So I snuggled in my chair.

Then I smelled something terrible
Just like some rotting meat.
I tracked it down and soon found out
It was my stinky feet.

I darted to the mirror
My suspicion made me frown.
My nose was running--my feet smelled
Yep, I AM built upside down.

Prickly Polly

Little Polly porcupine
Was always very slow,
And everytime she tried to walk
Her feet forgot to go.

She was a curious creature
But sometimes way too bold.
She would wander everywhere
When she was six weeks old.

Her brothers and her sisters
Walked in a nice straight row,
But she could not keep up with them
Cause her feet forgot to go.

She was the smallest one of all
And she knew how to talk.
She could chat her brothers ear off
But darned if she could walk.

One cloudy afternoon she found
That she had lost her way,
So with determination
Searched for her mom that day.

Now as her feet went backwards
She thought she'd found her past,
She bumped a cactus plant and squealed
"Wheee, I've found you mom at last."

Mixed Up Mess

Twinkle twinkle purple hog.
I'll dance the tango with my dog.

I'll sail a rowboat to the moon,
Then eat linguini with a spoon.

I'll serenade an alley cat,
Lounging in a cowboy hat.

Twinkle twinkle if I try,
Maybe I can see a big horse fly.

This poem is mixing up my head,

Goodnight,

I'm skating off to bed.

INDEX

Acknowledgements

Many thanks to those who helped in preparing this book:

Joyce Reese-- Your ideas, great skills and patience.
Dawn Humphries-- Those delightful, magical illustrations.
Merian Murphy-- Your expertise comments and suggestions.
Laurie Koelliker-- For your enthusiastic encouragement.
Jan Ruesch-- My husband who always loves and supports me.
James Ruesch-- For your generousity in making this book possible.

Peggy